W9-ASY-898

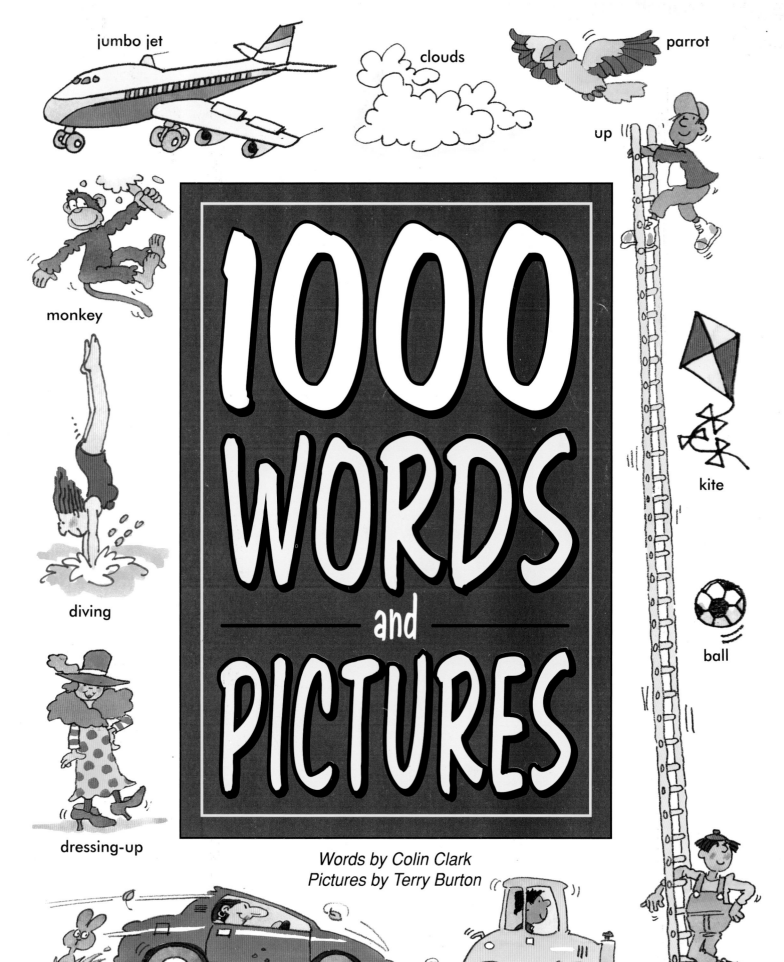

jumbo jet

clouds

parrot

up

monkey

kite

diving

ball

dressing-up

1000 WORDS and PICTURES

Words by Colin Clark
Pictures by Terry Burton

fast

slow

down

Brown Watson

ENGLAND

Contents

Page

4   Our Families and Ourselves

6   Our Bedroom

7   Our Bathroom

8   In Our Kitchen

10   The Living Room

11   Our Playroom

12   Our House and Garden

14   People at Work

16   Words in Action

18   Our Pets

20   At the Doctor

21   At the Dentist

22   Partytime

24   In the Park

26   In the Street

28   Builders and Buildings

30   At School

32   Games and Sports

34   In the Supermarket

36   Clothes to Wear

38   On the Farm

40   In the Country

42   On the Water

43   In the Garage

44   At the Railway Station

45   At the Airport

46   Wild Animals

48   All about Plants

50   At the Seaside

52   The Weather and the Seasons

54   In Storybooks

56   Opposites

57   Where are they?

58   Colours and Numbers

59   Shapes and Comparisons

60   Words in this Book

First published 1994 by Brown Watson. The Old Mill, 76 Fleckney Road, Kibworth Beauchamp, Leics, England
© 1994 Brown Watson
ISBN 0 7097 0970-8
Printed in Germany

Our Families and Ourselves

father/dad/husband

grandfather
(father's father)

hair

ear

face

grandmother
(father's mother)

daughter/
sister/girl

son/brother/boy

mouth

shoulder

tongue

lips

ankle

foot

toe

toes

fingers

chin

elbow

hand

thumb

4

mother/
mum/wife

grandmother
(mother's mother)

uncle (mother's brother)

eye

nose

finger

aunt
(mother's sister)

wrist

teeth

neck

arm

eyebrow

knee

leg

chest

head

Our Bedroom

wardrobe

bunk-beds

pillow

blanket

bed

duvet

sheet

chest of drawers

alarm clock

piggy bank

comb

lamp

quilt

coat-hanger

poster

rug

hairdryer

hairbrush

Our Bathroom

bath

bidet

bath mat

sink

shampoo

toilet

shower

towel

towel rail

sponge

tap

cabinet

razor

plug

scales

toothpaste

bubbles

7

In Our Kitchen

cooker

oven

plate

fork

knife

draining board

spoon

frying pan

washing machine

refrigerator

freezer

coffee-pot

apron

mop

broom

bottle

jug

socket

whisk

waste
bin

keys

saucepan

cup

saucer

kettle

plug

ironing board

iron

vacuum
cleaner

switch

jar

stool

brush

dustpan

food
mixer

egg

The Living Room

bookcase

footstool

screen

cushion

television

hi-fi

sofa

coffee table

books

fireplace

newspaper

video-recorder

table

chair

Our Playroom

building bricks

train set

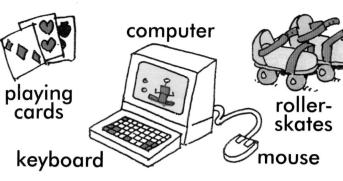
playing cards

computer

keyboard

mouse

roller-skates

dolls' pram

dolls' house

teddy bear

counting frame

toy car

dolls

paintbox

spinning-top

9

Our House and Garden

hedge

rake

lawn-mower

dustbin

lawn

ants

hoe

ladder

spade

wheelbarrow

compost heap

hose-pipe

gate

window

watering-can

front door

sprinkler

TV aerial

bees

roof tiles

porch

chimney

bonfire

window box

flowers

gutter

nesting box

drainpipe

roof

shed

greenhouse

bird table

trowel

caterpillar

snails

vegetables

13

People at Work

pilot

cook

firefighter

soldier

mechanic

gardener

bus driver

teacher

baker

builder

plumber

librarian

shop-assistant

painter and
decorator

vet

TV presenter

photographer

wrestler

cowboy

window-cleaner

postman

model

dancer

musician

police officer

sailor

air stewardess

woodworker

electrician

hairdresser

banker

clown

waiter

miner

tailor

judge

opera singer

Words in Action

a writer writing

a painter painting

standing up

lying down

kneeling

eating ice-cream

laughing

sneezing

watching T.V.

hiding

brushing the dog

throwing

hurrying

digging a hole

chopping wood

sewing

making

blowing a trumpet

16

marching

falling over

sitting down

a singer singing

a reader reading

drinking lemonade

crying

crawling

listening to the radio

saluting

catching

sweeping the floor

knitting

jumping

combing your hair

finding

cutting the grass

17

Our Pets

budgerigar

gerbils

cat-flap

fish tank

beak

birdcage

tortoise

cat's tail

puppies

mouse

pigeon's wing

goldfish

terrapins

water weed

rabbits

silkworms

toad

mouse's ears

kittens

hamsters

canary

parrot

perch

kennel

cat's paw

bird's claw

dog's bowl

play wheel

pony

horse's hoof

newt

stick insect

rabbit hutch

dove

mynah bird

bone

At the Doctor

torch

syringe

stethoscope

receptionist

bottle of medicine

couch

rubber hammer

doctor

prescription

medical books

height gauge

bottle of pills

eye chart

first-aid box

bandage

measuring beaker

filing cabinet

scales

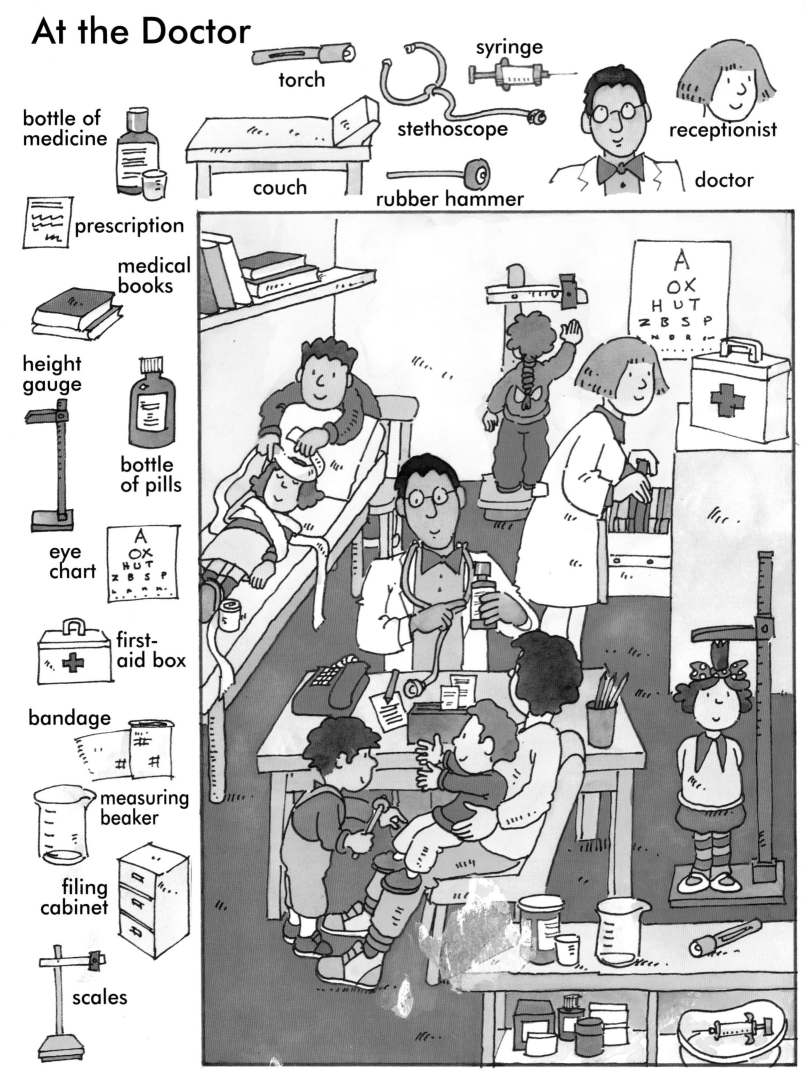

At the Dentist

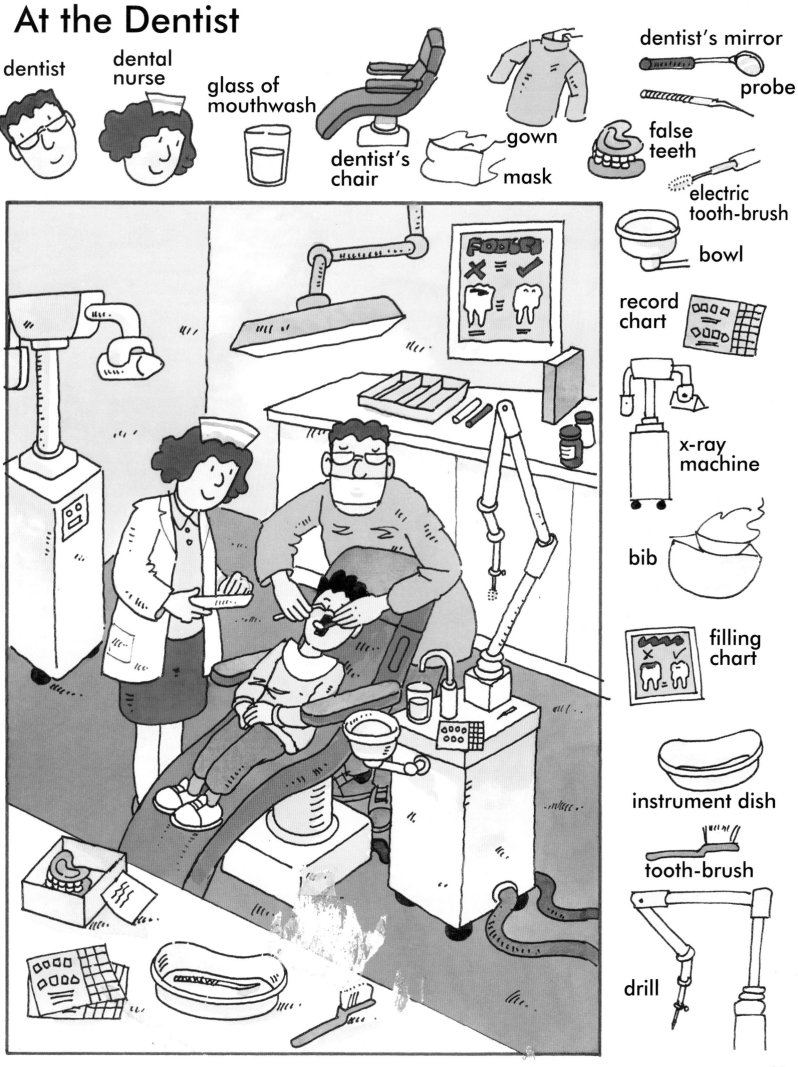

dentist

dental nurse

glass of mouthwash

dentist's chair

gown

mask

dentist's mirror

probe

false teeth

electric tooth-brush

bowl

record chart

x-ray machine

bib

filling chart

instrument dish

tooth-brush

drill

Partytime

busy grown-up

robot

thank-you kiss

lots of crumbs

jam doughnuts

broken toy

yo-yo

sparklers

fizzy drinks

birthday cards

HAPPY BIRTH DAY

sticky toffees

sandwich

balloons

candles

iced cake

drinking straws

PETE

JOHN PAT

22

paper hat

biscuit

magician's hat

cloak

cracker

magician

party invitation

jack-in-the-box

paper chain

crying child

jelly

nervous cat

xylophone

name tags

tablecloth

presents

23

In the Park

litter bin

spade

bucket

helmet

tadpoles

push-chair

see-saw

fountain

bicycle

swings

lead

frog

net

skateboard

pads

pigeons

collar

sand-pit

yacht

slide

drinking fountain

scooter

climbing frame

bandstand

wheelchair

duck

dog

muzzle

railings

notice board

skipping rope

kite

pond

roundabout

bench

In the Street

petrol pump

steam roller

police car

bank

digger

taxi

road

bus

kerb

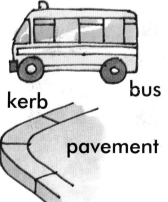
pavement

bicycle

telephone box

roundabout

motorist

signpost

car

shop

traffic lights

POST OFFICE

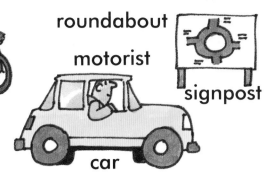

26

petrol station

streetlighting

attendant

breakdown lorry

motor-cyclist

pedestrian

post office

ambulance

statue

van

market

BANK

lorry

bus stop

fire engine

church

parking meter

traffic warden

postbox

Builders and Buildings

block of flats

hotel

theatre

crane

building site

bricks

hod

dump truck

safety helmet

scaffolding

bulldozer

cement mixer

navvy

factory

snack bar

bricklayer

terraced house

multi-storey car park

sports pavilion

cottage

tennis court

power station

28

office block

hospital

stately home

synagogue

church

police station

wooden hut

cinema

pub

school

ROXY

park

restaurant

playground

mosque

At School

shapes

pencil-case

slide projector

blackboard

chalk

teacher

desk

pencils

drawing pins

magnet

easel

wall chart

triangle

pot of paint

crayons

alphabet

abcdefg
hijklmn
opqrstu
vwxyz

pens

duster

globe

notebook

paper

pencil sharpener

calendar

school bus

modelling clay

satchel

model aircraft

writing

pot of paste

bell

paintbrush

sums $2+2=$ $4+4=$

lunch box

ruler

recorder

drawing

Games and Sports

diving-board

darts

tennis

football

ice skating

diving

baseball

skiing

golf

show-jumping

judo

leap-frog

cycling

table tennis

rowing

marbles

American football

32

archery

swimming

target

chess

ice hockey

cards

computer game

rugby

cricket

sailing

blind-man's buff

dressing-up

gymnastics

running

tug of war

riding

snooker

board game

In the Supermarket

credit card

fish

bread

shopping ba[g]

cashie[r]

cheese

slice

check-out

fruit juice

butter

eggs

ham

pie

money

tomatoes

lemons

bananas

mushrooms

carrots

34

washing
powder

spaghetti

till

receipt

trolley

breakfast
cereal

toilet rolls

chocolate bar

sausages

pears

oranges

apples

pineapple

potatoes

cucumber

cabbage

lettuce

Clothes to Wear

cap

gloves

anorak

jacket

t-shirt

underpants

vest

jumper

belt

trousers

shoes

pyjamas

sandals

socks

scarf

blouse

skirt

stockings

mittens

coat

raincoat

shirt

jeans

tracksuit

knickers/pants

tie

shorts

braces

tights

boots

night-dress

handkerchief

ribbon

dress

trainers

37

On the Farm

orchard

shepherd

goslings

pigsty

farmhouse

straw bales

stable

bull

horse

foal

barn

hen-house

cow

calf

wagon

milk tanker

hayloft

plough

farmer

farmer's wife

tractor

sheep-dog

horseshoe

lamb

sheep

duck

ducklings

turkey

kennel

piglet

pig

cockerel

milk churn

sacks

chicks

hen

In the Country

windmill

wild flowers

stepping stones

molehill

mole

forest

rowing-boat

hill

bridge

tent

fox

water mill

field

scarecrow

butterfly

hare

stream

waterfall

rucksack

lock

picnic

fox cubs

camp-fire

hiker

map

camper

sleeping bag

canoe

canal

mountains

houseboat

caravan

fishing rod

fisherman

barbecue

picnic basket

deer

41

On the Water

oil tanker

buoy

speedboat

stern   cruise liner   diving bell

bow

houseboat

barge

hydrofoil

paddle-steamer

ferry-boat

tug-boat

hover craft

submarine

mast

sail

yacht

In the Garage

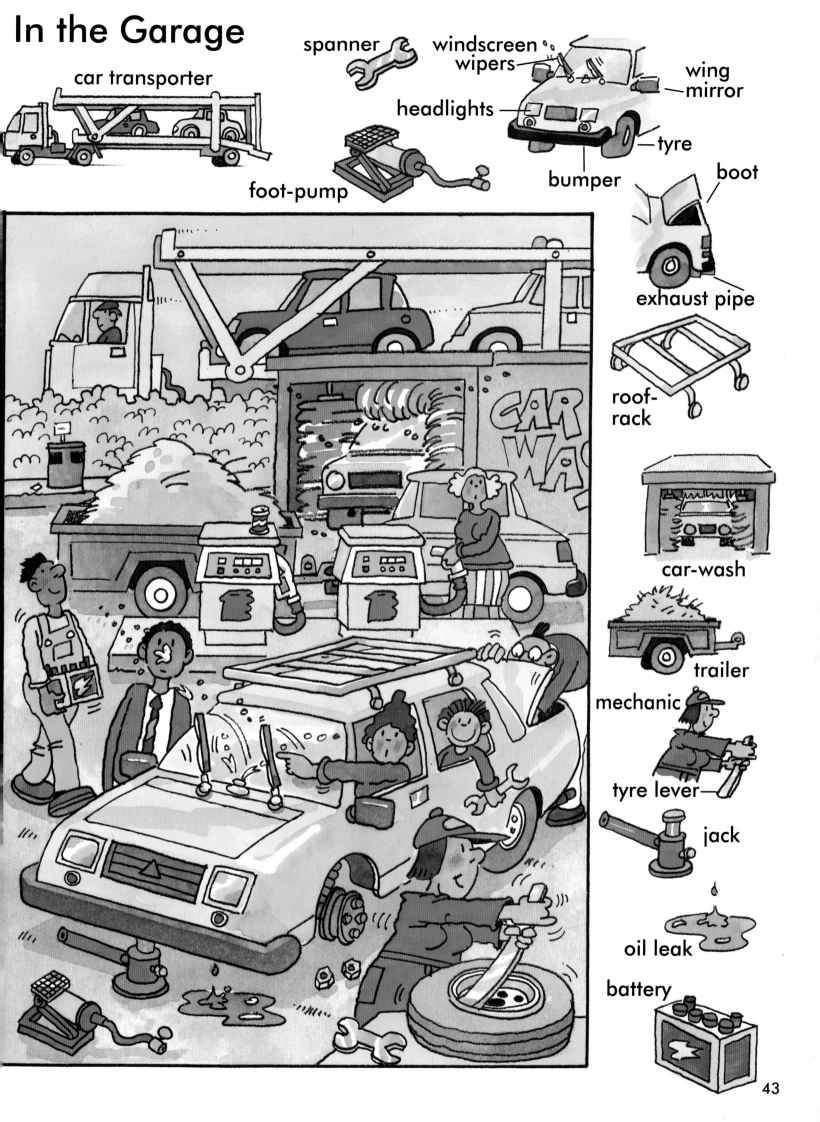

car transporter

spanner

windscreen wipers

headlights

wing mirror

tyre

bumper

boot

foot-pump

exhaust pipe

roof-rack

car-wash

trailer

mechanic

tyre lever

jack

oil leak

battery

CAR WASH

43

At the Railway Station

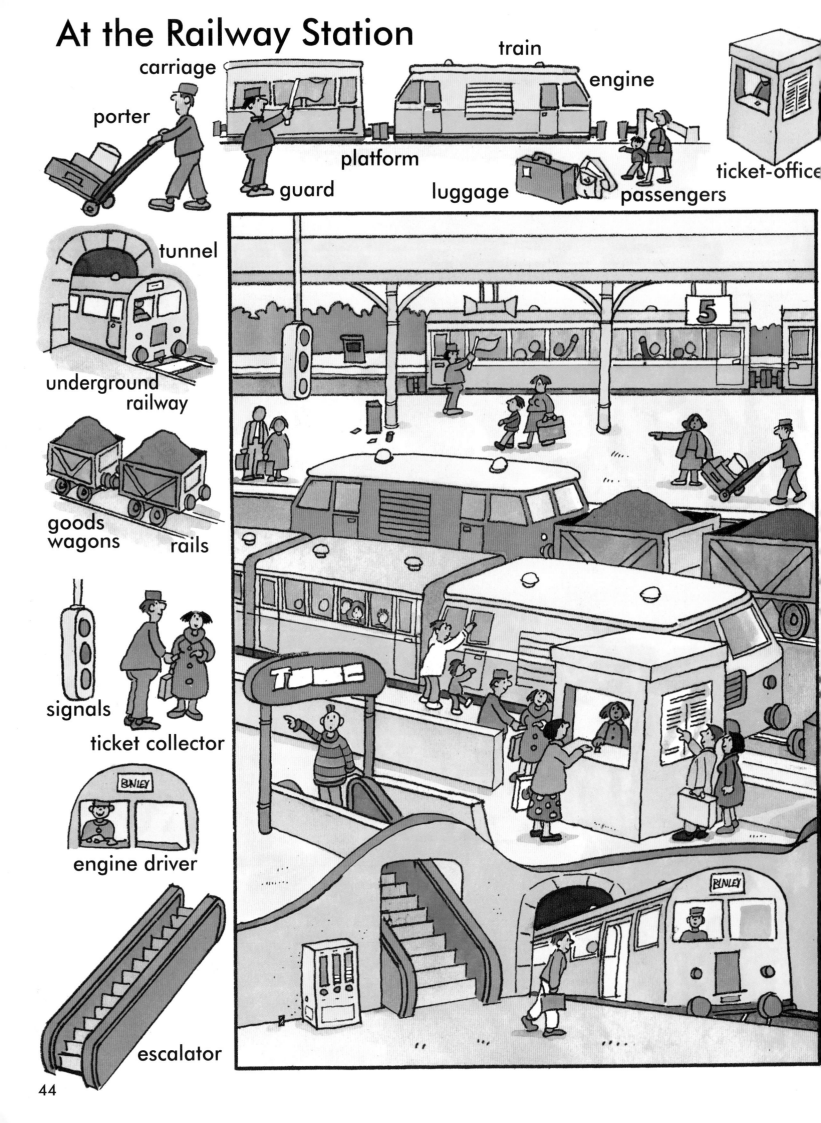

carriage

train

engine

porter

platform

guard

luggage

passengers

ticket-office

tunnel

underground railway

goods wagons

rails

signals

ticket collector

engine driver

escalator

At the Airport

Concorde

tail

jumbo jet

flap

wing

rotor blades

helicopter

control tower

seaplane

runway

glider

taking off

landing

light aircraft

propeller

fuel tanker

wind-sock

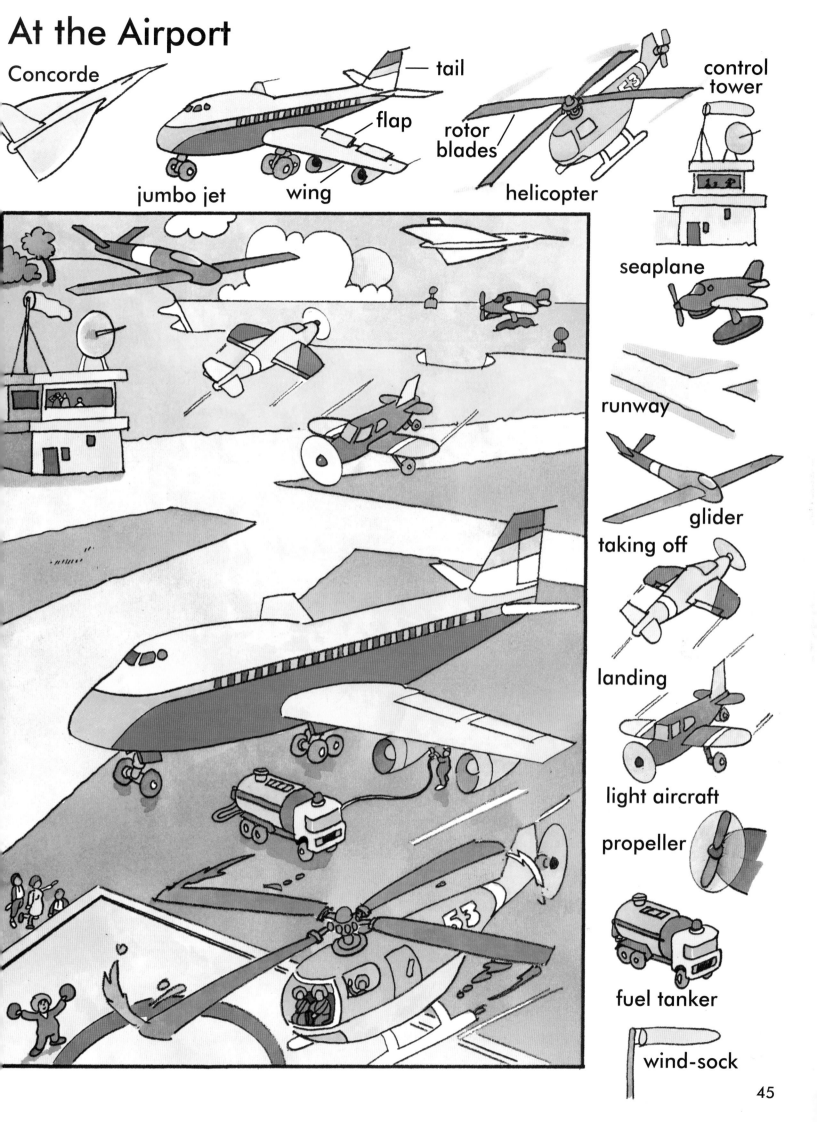

Wild Animals

hippopotamus (hippo)

panda

elephant

kangaroo

koala

dolphin

swordfish

giraffe

parrot

gorilla

peacock

wolf

walrus

lizard

hedgehog

lion

armadillo

leopard

swan

rhinoceros (rhino)

crocodile

zebra

platypus

whale

shark

octopus

ostrich

bat

camel

polar bear

monkey

tiger

seal

skunk

reindeer

badger

owl

cobra (a snake)

All about Plants

parts of a tree

twig

branch

leaf

bark

falling leaf

trunk

sapling

roots

fallen leaves

oak tree

fir tree

palm tree

monkey-puzzle tree

what grows on trees?

pine cone

chestnut

pineapple

apple

banana

coconut

mulberry

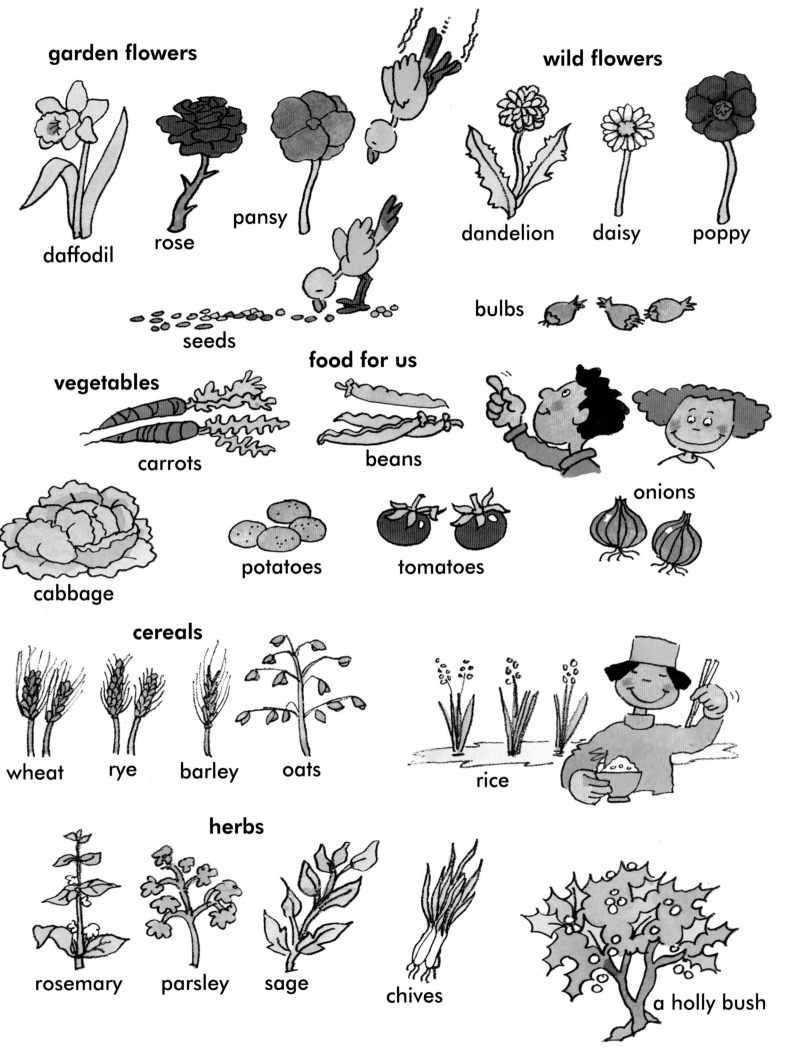

garden flowers

daffodil

rose

pansy

wild flowers

dandelion

daisy

poppy

seeds

bulbs

food for us

vegetables

carrots

beans

onions

cabbage

potatoes

tomatoes

cereals

wheat

rye

barley

oats

rice

herbs

rosemary

parsley

sage

chives

a holly bush

49

At the Seaside

splashing

crab

parasol

boatman

lighthouse

flippers

swimsuit

deckchair

seaweed

starfish

motor-boat

wind-surfer

rubber ring

sand-castle

inflatable boat

seagull

beach-mat

chain

anchor

fishing-boat

paddle

waves

beach

snorkel

pool

seashells

sunhat

sea-wall

beach-ball

jellyfish

water-skier

surfboard

pump

bollard

flag

The Weather and the Seasons

spring

summer

autumn

winter

clouds

fog

snow

ice

weather vane

flood

wind

storm

rainbow

dew

snowman

sunshine

weather house

rain

hail

frost

icicles

mud

lightning

gale

snowballs

toboggan

planting time

wind-sock

moonlight

weather chart

snowflakes

barometer

melting snowman

shadow

puddle

starry sky

In Storybooks

ghost

dragon

knight in armour

Santa

sleigh

sack of toys

reindeer

turret

castle

unicorn

crown

moat

drawbridge

giant

lovely princess

throne

queen

page-boy

spinning-wheel

mermaid

Where are they?

Colours and Numbers

a **white** whale

a **red** rose

a **blue** box

a **black** beetle

a **brown** button

a **green** grasshopper

an **orange** orange

a **yellow** yo-yo

a **pink** piglet

a **gold** goldfish

a **silver** slipper

a **purple** parachute

1 one whale

2 two beetles

3 three roses

4 four boxes
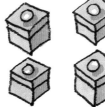

5 five yo-yos

6 six piglets

7 seven grasshoppers

8 eight buttons

9 nine goldfish

10 ten slippers

11 eleven parachutes

12 twelve oranges

Shapes and Comparisons

a square

a circle

an oval

a cube

a cone

a triangle

a star

a crescent

a diamond

a corner

a point

a straight line

a curved line

a toad

a bigger toad

the biggest toad

a long tail

a longer tail

the longest tail

little

less

the least

some

more

the most

a few sweets

fewer sweets

the fewest sweets

a giraffe

a taller giraffe

the tallest giraffe

Words in this Book

a

above	57
action	16
air stewardess	15
aircraft, light	45
aircraft, model	31
aircraft, toy	11
airport	45
alarm clock	6
alphabet	30
ambulance	27
American football	32
anchor	50
animals, wild	46
ankle	4
anorak	36
ants	12
apple	35, 48
apron	8
archery	33
arm	5
armadillo	46
armchair	10
armour, knight in	54
attendance	27
aunt	5
autumn	52

b

bad	56
badger	47
bag, shopping	34
bag, sleeping	41
baker	14
bales, straw	38
ball	24
balloons	22
banana	34, 48
bandage	20
bandstand	25
bank	26
bank, piggy	6
banker	15
bar, chocolate	35
bar, snack	28
barbecue	41
barge	42
bark	48
barley	49
barn	38
barometer	53
baseball	32
basket, picnic	41
bat	47
bath	7
bath mat	7
bathroom	7
battery	43
beach	51
beach-ball	51
beach-mat	50
beak	18
beaker, measuring	20

beans	49
bear, teddy	11
bed	6
bedroom	6
bees	13
beetle	58
behind	57
bell	31
bell, diving	42
below	57
belt	36
bench	25
between	57
bib	21
bicycle	24, 26
bidet	7
big	56
bigger	59
biggest	59
bin, litter	24
bin, waste	9
bird, mynah	19
bird table	13
bird's claw	19
birdcage	18
birthday cards	22
biscuit	23
black	58
blackboard	30
blades, rotor	45
blanket	6
blind-man's buff	33
block of flats	28
block, office	29
blouse	36
blowing a trumpet	16
blue	58
board game	33
board, draining	8
board, notice	25
board, ironing	9
boat, inflatable	50
boatman	50
bollard	51
bone	19
bonfire	13
bookcase	10
books	10
books, medical	20
boot	37, 43
bottle	8
bottle of medicine	20
bottle of pills	20
bow	42
bowl	19, 21
box	58
box, first-aid	20
box, lunch	31
box, nesting	13
box, telephone	26
box, window	13
boy	5
braces	37

branch	48
bread	34
breakdown lorry	27
breakfast cereal	35
bricklayer	28
bricks	11, 28
bridge	40
broken toy	22
broom	8
broomstick	55
brother	5
brown	58
brush	9
brushing the dog	16
bubbles	7
bucket	24
budgerigar	18
builder	14, 28
building bricks	11
building site	28
buildings	28
bulbs	49
bull	38
bulldozer	28
bumper	43
bunk-bed	6
buoy	42
buried treasure	55
bus	26
bus driver	14
bus stop	15
bus, school	31
bush, holly	49
busy grown-up	22
butter	34
butterfly	40
button	58

c

cabbage	35, 49
cabinet	7
cabinet, filing	20
cake, iced	22
calendar	31
calf	38
camel	47
camp-fire	41
camper	41
canal	41
canary	19
candles	22
canoe	41
cap	36
car	26
car-wash	43
car park	28
car transporter	43
car, police	26
car, toy	11
caravan	41
card, credit	34
cards	33
carpet, magic	55

carriage	44
carrots	34, 49
cashier	34
castle	54
cat, nervous	23
cat's paw	19
cat's tail	18
cat-flap	18
catching	17
caterpillar	13
cauldron, witch's	55
cement mixer	28
cereal, breakfast	35
cereals	49
chain	50
chain, paper	23
chair	10
chalk	30
chart, filling	21
chart, record	21
chart, wall	30
chart, weather	53
check-out	34
cheese	34
chess	33
chest	5
chest of drawers	6
chestnut	48
chicks	39
child, crying	23
chimney	13
chin	4
chives	49
chocolate bar	35
chopping wood	16
church	27, 29
churn, milk	39
cinema	29
circle	59
claw, bird's	19
clay, modelling	31
clean	56
cleaner, vacuum	9
climbing frame	25
cloak	23
clock, alarm	6
clothes	36
clouds	52
clown	15
coat	37
coat-hanger	6
cobra	47
cockerel	39
coconut	48
coffee-pot	8
coffee table	10
collar	24
collector, ticket	44
colours	58
comb	6
combing hair	17
comparisons	59
compost heap	12

computer	11
computer game	33
Concorde	45
cone	59
cone, pine	48
control tower	45
cook	14
cooker	8
corner	59
cottage	28
couch	20
counting frame	11
country	40
court, tennis	28
cow	38
cowboy	14
crab	50
cracker	23
crane	28
crawling	17
crayons	30
credit card	34
crescent	59
cricket	33
crocodile	47
crown	54
cruise liner	42
crying	17
crying child	23
cube	59
cubs, fox	41
cucumber	35
cup	9
curved	59
cushion	10
cutting grass	17
cycling	32

d

dad	4
daffodil	49
daisy	49
dancer	15
dandelion	49
darts	32
daughter	4
deckchair	50
decorator	14
deer	41
dental nurse	21
dentist	21
dentist's chair	21
dentist's mirror	21
desk	30
dew	52
diamond	59
difficult	56
digger	26
digging a hole	16
dirty	56
diving	32
diving bell	42
diving-board	32
doctor	20
dog	25

dog, brushing	16
dog's bowl	19
dolls	11
dolls' house	11
dolls' pram	11
dolphin	46
door, front	12
dove	19
down	57
dragon	54
draining board	8
drainpipe	13
drawbridge	54
drawing	31
drawing pins	30
dress	37
dressing-up	33
drill	21
drinking fountain	25
drinking lemonade	17
drinking straws	22
drinks, fizzy	22
driver, engine	44
dry	56
duck	25, 39
ducklings	39
dump truck	28
dustbin	12
duster	30
dustpan	9
duvet	6
dwarfs	55

e

ear	4
easel	30
easy	56
eating ice-cream	16
egg-cup	9
eggs	34
eight	58
elbow	4
electric tooth-brush	21
electrician	15
elephant	46
eleven	58
engine	44
engine driver	44
engine, fire	27
escalator	44
exhaust pipe	43
eye	5
eye chart	20
eyebrow	5

f

face	4
factory	28
fairy	55
fallen leaves	48
falling leaf	48
falling over	17
false teeth	21
families	4
far	57
farm	38

farmer	39
farmer's wife	39
farmhouse	38
fast	56
fat	56
father	4
ferry-boat	42
few	59
fewer	59
fewest	59
field	40
filing cabinet	20
filling chart	21
finding	17
finger	5
fingers	4
fir tree	48
fire engine	27
firefighter	14
fireplace	10
first	57
first-aid box	20
fish	34
fish tank	18
fisherman	41
fishing-boat	51
fishing rod	41
five	58
fizzy drinks	22
flag	51, 55
flap	45
flats, block of	28
flippers	50
flood	52
floor, sweeping	17
flowers	13, 49
flowers, garden	49
flowers, wild	49
flying horse	55
foal	38
fog	52
food	49
food-mixer	9
foot	4
foot-pump	43
football	32
football, American	32
footstool	10
forest	40
fork	8
fountain	24, 25
fountain, drinking	25
four	58
fox	40
fox cubs	41
frame, climbing	25
frame, counting	11
freezer	8
frog	24
front	57
front door	12
frost	53
fruit juice	34
frying pan	8
fuel tanker	45

g

gale	53
game, board	33
game, computer	33
games	32
garage	43
garden	12
garden flowers	49
gardener	14
gate	12
gerbils	18
ghost	54
giant	54
giraffe	46, 59
girl	4
glass of mouthwash	21
glider	45
globe	31
gloves	36
gold	58
goldfish	18, 58
golf	32
good	56
goods wagons	44
gorilla	46
goslings	38
gown	21
grandfather	4
grandmother	4, 5
grass, cutting	17
grasshopper	58
green	58
greenhouse	13
grown-up	22
grows	48
guard	44
gutter	13
gymnastics	33

h

hail	53
hair	4
hair, combing	17
hairbrush	6
hairdresser	15
hairdryer	6
ham	34
hammer, rubber	20
hamsters	19
hand	4
handkerchief	37
handsome prince	55
happy	56
hare	40
hat, magician's	23
hat, paper	23
hayloft	38
head	5
headlights	43
heap, compost	12
hedge	12
hedgehog	46
height gauge	20
helicopter	45
helmet	24

helmet, safety 28
hen 39
hen-house 38
hi-fi 10
hiding 16
high 57
hiker 41
hill 40
hippopotamus (hippo) 46
hod 28
hoe 12
hole, digging 16
holly bush 49
home, stately 29
hoof, horse's 19
horse 38
horse, flying 55
horse's hoof 19
horseshoe 39
hose-pipe 12
hospital 29
hotel 28
house 12
house, dolls' 11
house, terraced 28
house, weather 52
houseboat 41, 42
hovercraft 42
hurrying 16
husband 4
hut, wooden 29
hutch, rabbit 19
hydrofoil 42

i

ice 52
ice-cream, eating 16
ice hockey 33
ice skating 32
iced cake 22
icicles 53
in 57
in front 57
inflatable boat 50
insect, stick 19
instrument dish 21
invitation, party 23
iron 9
ironing board 9

j

jack 43
jack-in-the-box 23
jacket 36
jam doughnuts 22
jar 9
jeans 37
jelly 23
jellyfish 51
jet, jumbo 45
judge 15
judo 32
jug 8
juice, fruit 34
jumbo jet 45

jumper 36
jumping 17

k

kangaroo 46
kennel 19, 39
kerb 26
kettle 9
keyboard 11
keys 9
king 55
kiss, thank-you 22
kitchen 8
kite 25
kittens 19
knee 5
kneeling 16
knickers (pants) 37
knife 8
knight in armour 54
knitting 17
koala 46

l

ladder 12
lamb 39
lamp 6
landing 45
last 57
laughing 16
lawn 12
lawn-mower 12
lead 24
leaf, leaves 48
leak, oil 43
leap-frog 32
least 59
left 57
leg 5
lemonade, drinking 17
lemons 34
leopard 46
less 59
lettuce 35
lever, tyre 43
librarian 14
light aircraft 45
lights, traffic 26
lighthouse 50
lightning 53
line 59
liner, cruise 42
lion 46
lips 4
listening to the radio 17
litter bin 24
little 59
living room 10
lizard 46
lock 40
long 59
longer 59
longest 59
lorry, breakdown 27
lots of crumbs 22

lovely princess 54
low 57
luggage 44
lunch box 31
lying down 16

m

machine, washing, 8
machine, x-ray 21
magic carpet 55
magic wand 55
magician 23
magician's hat 23
magnet 30
making 16
map 41
marbles 32
marching 17
market 27
mask 21
mast 42
mat, bath 7
measuring beaker 20
mechanic 14, 43
medicine 20
melting snowman 53
mermaid 54
meter, parking 27
milk churn 39
milk tanker 38
mill, water 40
miner 15
mirror, wing 43
mittens 37
mixer, cement 28
moat 54
model 15
model aircraft 31
modelling clay 31
mole 40
molehill 40
money 34
monkey-puzzle tree 48
moonlight 53
mop 8
more 59
mosque 29
most 59
mother 5
motor-boat 50
motor-cyclist 27
motorist 26
mountains 41
mouse (computer) 11
mouse (pet) 18
mouse's ears 18
mouth 4
mud 53
mulberry 48
multi-storey car park 29
mum 5
mushrooms 34
musician 15
muzzle 25
mynah bird 19

n

name tags 23
navvy 28
near 57
neck 5
nervous cat 23
nesting box 13
net 24
newspaper 10
newt 19
night-dress 37
nine 58
nose 5
notebook 31
notice board 25
numbers 58
nurse, dental 21

o

oak tree 48
oats 49
octopus 47
office block 29
office, post 27
oil leak 43
oil tanker 42
one 58
onions 49
opera singer 15
opposites 56
orange 58
oranges 35
orchard 38
ostrich 47
ourselves 4
out 57
oval 59
oven 8
over 57
owl 47

p

paddle 51
paddle-steamer 42
pads 24
page-boy 54
paint, pot of 30
paint-box 11
paintbrush 31
painter 14, 16
painting 16
palace 55
palm tree 48
panda 46
pansy 49
pants (knickers) 37
paper 31
paper chain 23
paper hat 23
parachute 58
parasol 50
park 24, 29
parking meter 27
parrot 19, 46
parsley 49

parts of a tree	48	post office	27	roof	13	shapes	30, 59
party invitation	23	postbox	27	roof-rack	43	shark	47
partytime	22	poster	6	roof tiles	13	sharpener, pencil	31
passengers	44	postman	15	roots	48	shed	13
paste, pot of	31	pot of paint	30	rope, slipping	25	sheep	39
pavement	26	pot of paste	31	rose	49, 58	sheep-dog	39
pavilion, sports	28	potatoes	35, 49	rosemary	49	sheet	6
paw, cat's	19	powder, washing	35	rotor, blades	45	shepherd	38
peacock	46	power station	28	roundabout (park)	25	shirt	37
pears	35	pram, dolls	11	roundabout (road)	26	shoes	36
pedestrian	27	prescription	20	rowing	32	shop	26
pencil-case	30	presents	23	rowing-boat	40	shop-assistant	14
pencil sharpener	31	prince, handsome	55	rubber hammer	20	shopping bag	34
pencils	30	princess, lovely	54	rubber ring	50	shorts	37
pens	30	probe	21	rucksack	40	shoulder	4
people	14	projector, slide	30	rug	6	show-jumping	32
perch	19	propeller	45	rugby	33	shower	7
petrol pump	26	pub	29	ruler	31	signals	44
petrol station	27	puddle	53	running	33	signpost	26
pets	18	pump	51	runway	45	silkworms	18
photographer	14	pump, petrol	26	rye	49	silver	58
photographs	10	puppet	11			singer	17
picnic	41	puppies	18	**s**		singer, opera	15
picnic basket	41	purple	58	sack of toys	54	singing	17
picture	10	push-chair	24	sacks	39	sink	7
pie	34	pyjamas	36	sad	56	sister	4
pig	39			safety helmet	28	sitting down	17
pigeon's wing	18	**q**		sage	49	six	58
pigeons	24	queen	54	sail	42	skateboard	24
piggy bank	6	quilt	6	sailing	33	skating, ice	32
piglet	39, 58			sailor	15	skiing	32
pigsty	38	**r**		saluting	17	skipping rope	25
pillow	6	rabbit hutch	19	sand-castle	50	skirt	36
pills	20	rabbits	18	sand-pit	24	skull and crossbones	55
pilot	14	radio, listening	17	sandals	36	skunk	47
pine cone	48	rail, towel	7	sandwich	22	sky, starry	53
pineapple	35, 48	railings	25	Santa	54	sleeping bag	41
pink	58	rails	44	sapling	48	sleigh	54
pins, drawing	30	railway station	44	satchel	31	slice	34
pipe, exhaust	58	railway, underground	44	saucepan	9	slide	25
pirate	55	rain	53	saucer	9	slide projector	30
planting time	53	rainbow	52	sausages	35	slipper	58
plants	48	raincoat	37	scaffolding	28	slow	56
plate	8	rake	12	scales	7, 20	small	56
platform	44	razor	7	scarecrow	40	snack bar	28
platypus	47	reader	17	scarf	36	snails	13
play wheel	19	reading	17	school	29, 30	snake	47
playground	29	receipt	35	school bus	31	sneezing	16
playroom	11	receptionist	20	scooter	25	snooker	33
playing cards	11	record chart	21	screen	10	snorkel	51
plough	39	recorder	31	sea-wall	51	snow	52
plug (electric)	9	red	58	seagull	50	snowballs	53
plug (sink)	7	refrigerator	8	seal	47	snowflakes	53
plumber	14	reindeer	47, 54	seaplane	45	snowman	52, 53
point	59	restaurant	29	seashells	51	socket	8
polar bear	47	rhinoceros (rhino)	47	seaside	50	socks	36
police car	26	ribbon	37	seasons	52	sofa	10
police officer	15	rice	49	seaweed	50	soft toys	11
police station	29	riding	33	see-saw	24	soldier	14
pond	25	right	57	seeds	49	some	59
pony	19	road	26	seven	58	son	4
pool	51	robot	22	seven dwarfs	55	spade	12, 24
poppy	49	rod, fishing	41	sewing	16	spaghetti	35
porch	13	roller-skates	11	shadow	53	spanner	43
porter	44	roller, steam	26	shampoo	7	sparklers	22

speedboat	42	tags, name	23	tractor	39
spinning-top	11	tail	45, 59	traffic lights	26
spinning-wheel	54	tail, cat's	18	traffic warden	27
splashing	50	tailor	15	trailer	43
sponge	7	taking off	45	train	44
spoon	8	taller	59	train set	11
sports	32	tallest	59	trainers	37
sports pavilion	28	tank, fish	18	transporter, car	43
spring	52	tanker, fuel	45	treasure, buried	55
sprinkler	13	tanker, milk	38	tree	48
square	59	tanker, oil	42	tree, fir	48
stable	38	tap	7	tree, monkey-puzzle	48
standing up	16	target	33	tree, oak	48
star	59	taxi	26	tree, palm	48
starfish	50	teacher	14, 30	triangle	30, 59
starry sky	53	teddy bear	11	trolley	35
stately home	29	teeth	5	trousers	36
station, petrol	27	teeth, false	21	trowel	13
station, police	29	telephone	10	truck, dump	28
station, power	28	telephone box	26	trumpet, blowing	16
station, railway	44	television	10	trunk	48
statue	27	ten	58	tug-boat	42
steam roller	26	tennis	32	tug-of-war	33
stepping stones	40	tennis court	28	tunnel	44
stern	42	tent	40	turkey	39
stethoscope	20	terraced house	28	turret	54
stick insect	19	terrapins	18	TV aerial	13
sticky toffees	22	thank-you kiss	22	TV presenter	14
stockings	36	theatre	28	TV, watching	16
stones, stepping	40	thin	56	twelve	58
stool	9	three	58	twig	48
stop, bus	27	throne	54	two	58
storm	52	throwing	16	tyre	43
storybooks	54	thumb	4	tyre lever	43
straight	59	ticket collector	44		
straw bales	38	ticket-office	44	**U**	
straws, drinking	22	tidy	56	uncle	5
stream	40	tie	37	under	57
street	26	tiger	47	underground railway	44
streetlighting	27	tights	37	underpants	36
submarine	42	tiles, roof	13	unicorn	54
summer	52	till	35	untidy	56
sums	31	time, planting	53	up	57
sunhat	51	toad	18, 59	us	49
sunshine	52	toboggan	53		
supermarket	34	toe, toes	5	**V**	
surfboard	51	toffees, sticky	22	vacuum cleaner	9
swan	46	toilet	7	van	27
sweeping the floor	17	toilet rolls	35	vane, weather	52
swimming	33	tomatoes	34, 49	vegetables	13, 49
swimsuit	50	tongue	4	vest	36
swings	24	tooth-brush	21	vet	14
switch	9	tooth-brush, electric	21	video-recorder	10
swordfish	46	toothpaste	7		
synagogue	29	torch	20	**W**	
syringe	20	tortoise	18	wagon	38
		towel	7	wagons, goods	44
t		towel rail	7	waiter	15
t-shirt	36	tower, control	45	wall chart	30
table	10	toy aircraft	11	walrus	46
table, bird	13	toy car	11	wand, magic	55
table, coffee	10	toy, broken	22	warden, traffic	27
table tennis	32	toys, sack of	54	wardrobe	6
tablecloth	23	toys, soft	11	washing machine	8
tadpoles	24	tracksuit	37	washing powder	35
				waste bin	9

watching TV	16
water	42
water mill	40
water-skier	51
water weed	18
waterfall	40
watering-can	12
waves	51
wear	36
weather	52
weather chart	53
weather house	52
weather vane	52
wet	56
whale	47, 58
wheat	49
wheel, play	19
wheelbarrow	12
wheelchair	19
where	57
whisk	9
white	58
wife	5
wife, farmer's	39
wild animals	46
wild flowers	49
wind	52
wind-sock	45, 53
wind-surfer	50
windmill	40
window	12
window box	13
window-cleaner	15
windscreen wipers	43
wing	45
wing mirror	43
wing, pigeon's	18
winter	52
wishing-well	55
witch	55
witch's cauldron	55
wizard	55
wolf	46
wood, chopping	16
wooden hut	29
woodworker	15
words	16
work	14
wrestler	14
wrist	5
writer	16
writing	16, 31
x	
x-ray machine	21
xylophone	23
y	
yacht	25, 42
yellow	58
yo-yo	22, 58
z	
zebra	47